363
S 386

HAWKEYE COMMUNITY COLLEGE

W9-BNG-691

WITHDRAWN

Guns
What You Should Know

Rachel Ellenberg Schulson • illustrations by Mary Jones

Albert Whitman & Company • Morton Grove, Illinois

363 S386
Schulson, Rachel Ellenberg
Guns : what you should know
ocm500671866

HAWKEYE COMM. COLLEGE LIBRARY
Waterloo, Iowa

Library of Congress Cataloging-in-Publication Data

Schulson, Rachel Ellenberg.
Guns: what you should know / written by Rachel Ellenberg
Schulson ; illustrated by Mary Jones.
p.   cm.
Summary: Describes different kinds of guns, explains how they
are used, warns of possible dangers they present, and spells out
simple rules to ensure gun safety.

ISBN 0-8075-3093-X
1. Gun control—United States.
2. Firearms—United States—Safety measures.
[1. Gun Control. 2. Firearms—Safety measures. 3. Safety.]
I. Jones, Mary, ill. II. Title.
HV7436.S384 1997
363.3'3—dc21
97-7566
CIP
AC

For Henry, Michael, and Leah with love,
and to Kim, for helping me see it.
—R. S.

For CJM and JCD.
—M. J.

Most children play with toy guns or use their hands to pretend they are holding a gun. In the summertime, maybe you cool off by shooting water guns with a friend. Have you ever wondered about real guns?

Rifles and shotguns are two of the many kinds of guns. These long guns are called shoulder arms because they are held up to the shoulder when firing.

Pistols and revolvers are shorter than shoulder arms. They are called handguns because they can be held and fired with one or both hands.

What makes the bullet go flying out of the gun in such a hurry? Pulling the trigger starts a series of movements inside the gun which ends up with an explosion of gunpowder and a loud boom. That explosion sends the bullet on its way. All of this takes less than a second.

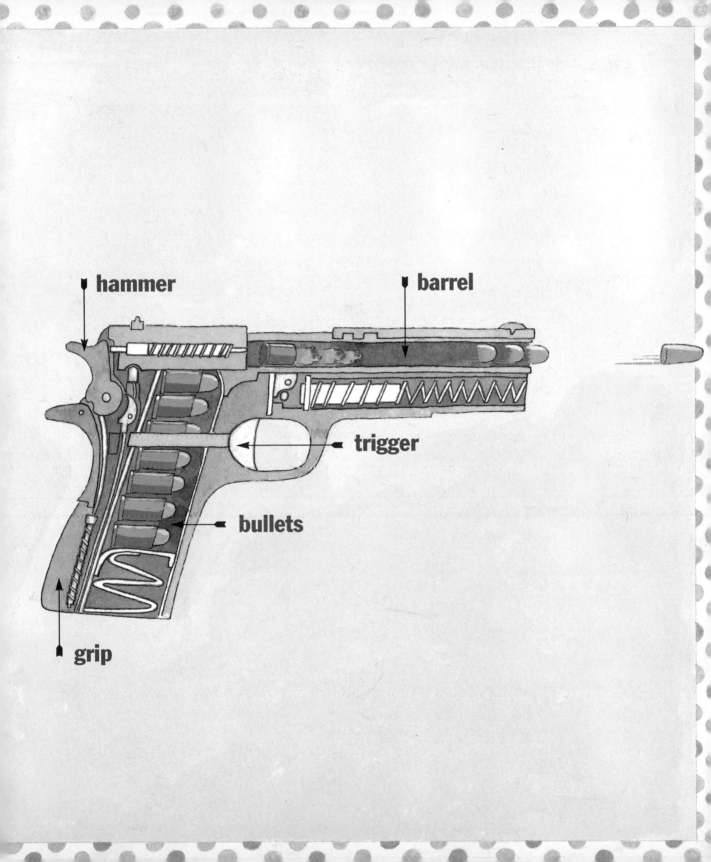

hammer

barrel

trigger

bullets

grip

A bullet shot from a gun can travel up to 5,000 feet per second. That means that if you and a bullet had a race, the bullet would get to the end of your block before you even took your first step.

FINISH

A bullet will keep going until it hits something. If a gun is shot at a wall, the bullet will make a hole in the wall. Maybe it will stop somewhere inside the wall. Or it might travel through the wall and come out the other side.

It is impossible to know exactly where the bullet will end up.

You have probably heard that guns are dangerous. When you see shooting in the movies or on TV, you might not realize how badly a gun can hurt someone.

A person who has been hit by a bullet can be in awful
pain, or perhaps become blind or unable to move his or
her legs. A gunshot wound can even kill a person.

In this country, there are laws about who can have a gun and where guns can be carried. Some people think that there should be stricter laws. Other people think that our laws about guns should be less strict. People in each of these groups feel strongly that they are right. They often argue about gun laws.

No matter how they feel about guns, all grownups agree on one thing: Children should never play with guns! Each year in the United States, about 200 children are killed from accidents with guns. Many of these children might not have died if they had known more about gun safety.

There are things you can do to protect yourself and other children from harm. Turn the page to find out how.

Rules

If you ever find a gun:

1. Don't guess that it's a toy gun. Treat it like it's real and stay away!

2. Leave the room and find a grownup. Do not stay near a child who is touching a gun. A bullet might end up in *you*. Find a grownup quickly so your friend doesn't get hurt, either.

3. Never let anyone aim a gun at you, even if that person says the gun isn't loaded. People make mistakes.